THE LOVE STORY OF
SUSHI & SASHIMI

A CAT TALE

Photographs by
SuZen

Story by
John Daniel

Lois —

Thanks for everything !

♡ SuZen

CAPRA PRESS
SANTA BARBARA

Design by Cyndi Burt and SuZen
Author's photo by Barbara Loudis

Published by Capra Press
P.O. Box 2068, Santa Barbara, CA 93120

If you are interested in other
books for cat lovers, please
call or write for a free catalog.

CAPRA PRESS
P.O. Box 2068, Santa Barbara, CA 93120
(805)966-4590

LIBRARY OF CONGRESS CATALOGING IN PUBLICATION DATA
SuZen 1946-
        The love story of Sushi & Sashimi: a cat tale / photographs
by SuZen ; story by John Daniel.
    p.   cm.
ISBN 0-88496-317-9 (paper) : $9.95
  1. Photography of cats. 2. Cats--Pictorial works. 3. Cats--Anecdotes.
  4. SuZen, 1946-   . I. Daniel, John, 1941 Nov. 21
  II. Title. III. Title: Sushi & Sashimi. IV. Title: Sushi and
  Sashimi.
  TR729.C3S8   1990
  779'.32--dc20   90-36306 CIP

Foreword

If it is true that cats choose their "owners," then I am truly fortunate to have been chosen by Sushi and Sashimi. They are my entertainment, and they are my teachers, and I am grateful to them for gracing my home with their presence.

Sushi arrived first, and he came in a professional capacity. I had a mouse problem, and a friend of mine loaned me her cat to take care of business. Sushi entered my apartment and got right to work; within twenty minutes he had nabbed the first of many mice, and we agreed that he would stay on retainer for free room and board for a week. It was a successful arrangement; Sushi obviously had a taste for that kind of work, and he completed the job with relish.

That summer Sushi's "owner" had plans to be out of town for two months, so Sushi came to stay with me again. He made himself completely at home, and made my home his. When his "owner" returned—after two years instead of two months—she could see right away that Sushi now "belonged" to me, and I to him. We were made for each other, and all three of us knew that Sushi had moved in with me for keeps. Whether I was keeping him or vice versa is a question we never addressed. But it was, and still is, a good hand-to-mouse relationship.

Our only problem had to do with possessiveness. Sushi did not like being left alone; whereas I'm independent enough to want to get out of the apartment every now and then. He allowed me to leave, but then he'd punish me with a surly voice when I got back, and even would bat me around a bit. So I had to face my own possessiveness and get Sushi a companion. A lady friend.

Enter Sashimi, a beautiful, if shy, twelve-week-old.

My first effort as a matchmaker was hardly an instant success. I pushed her forward, this timid little blue-eyed ball of fur, expecting Sushi to bow, take her paw, and escort her around her new home. Instead he swatted her, spit at her, and howled for her to get out of his apartment.

The following few weeks were not easy for any of us. A lot of yelling, a lot of chasing, a lot of sulking, a lot of ungentlemanly behavior, and not much ladylike behavior either. I won't go into details. Let's just say I give Sashimi a lot of credit for being persistent.

And then one day I came home and there were no cats in sight. I looked everywhere, fearing that my apartmentmates had chased each other out of existence. Finally I found them on the highest shelf, sleeping together on top of my backpack. Sushi opened one blue eye, and Sashimi opened another, and then they closed their eyes and resumed purring.

The Siamese education of Sushi and Sashimi has been my education as well. I have learned much from these two: about love, about life, about territory, and about dignity and play. I invite you to have a look into their very private lives.

To begin with, I wasn't sure it was a good idea. When she first arrived—frightened, ridiculously young and foolish—I thought: This is not going to work out.

Besides, one cat is plenty. This apartment is mine, and mine alone.

Nice try, but no thanks.

Well of course I was frightened. Taken from my warm, purring litter, carried in a cage through the loud city streets, plopped down in a strange-smelling apartment...I was terrified.

And then I saw him, and I knew: My master and teacher. My playmate and companion and friend. Another cat.

I knew I'd come home for good.

For good?
Forget it.

She'll never make it, and I have my reputation to consider.

Of course it took a little work convincing him he needed me as much as I needed him. He was the old hand, the bigshot, and he knew all there was to know about poise, and dignity, how to hold his tail, and how to yell for food in Siamese. Clearly he saw himself as the "Master."

But what did the "Master" know of love? Of sleeping together in a warm knot, of delicate kisses on the nose, of a fast chase through the land of mischief?

This arrogant teenager—she didn't realize, of course, that I'd long since forgotten more mischief than she'd ever learned.

But I had to admit she was cute. So I took her on as a pupil. She had a long way to go, but she had possiblities.

It was those kisses on the nose that did it..

And so the lessons began.

I started her on the Martial Arts: I taught her the Law of Fang and Claw. I taught her to wrestle and reach. When she could reach, she could stand on two legs.

And when I was sure she could stand, I taught my pupil to fly.

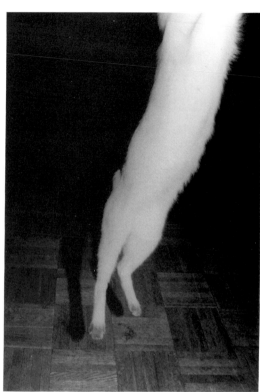
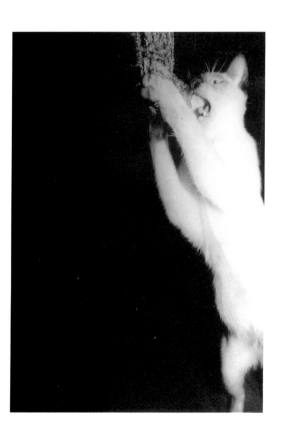

wonder if my Master knows, even now, that while he was teaching me to wrestle I was teaching him to love.

Then, when she was ready, I taught her Exploring and Investigation. There's a World Outside and a World Inside, and a proper Siamese needs to know both.

As for the World Outside, where there's a willful cat there's a way out.

For the World Inside, there are no words, only the Wisdom that purrs…

… **a** nd the Wisdom that plays.

SASHIMI

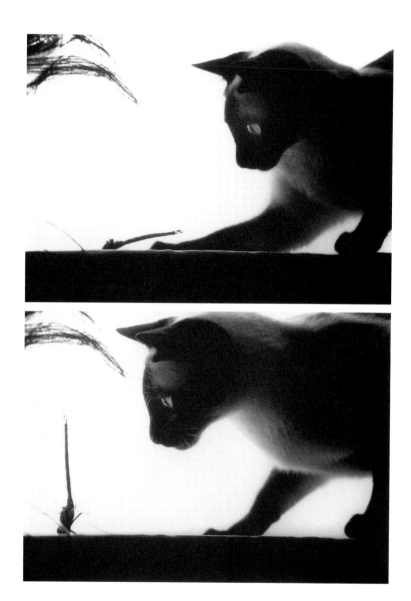

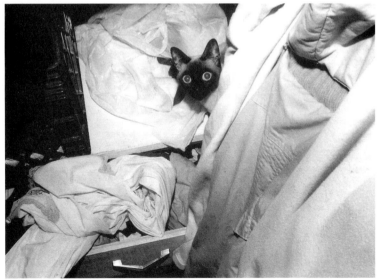

inally, when Sashimi had attained her Black Paws, I taught her the Noble Positions. Sitting. Standing. The Many Ways of lying Siamese. She learned them all and she learned them well.

She was, and is, a good pupil.

Just look at that tail.

And Sushi is the perfect Master.

Like all good teachers, although he's far too proud to admit it, he has learned too. He gave me lessons in dignity and grace and poise. I shook up his world and gave him the chase, the kiss, the partnership of sleeping in knots, and the knowledge of the fundamental Siamese Truth: Balance.

It's true. I too have learned.

where there's a Yang…

... *t* *here's a Yin.*

SASHIMI